CW00435663

L O W

A collection of delicious easy-to-make recipes

Contents

Text by Sara Burford.
Originally published in 2008 by L&K Designs. This edition published my Myriad Books Limited.
© L&K Designs 2008
PRINTED IN CHINA

Publishers Disclaimer

The recipes contained in this book are passed on in good faith but the publisher cannot be held responsible for any adverse results. Please be aware that certain recipes may contain nuts.

Introduction

Anyone with even the smallest amount of interest in their health will know that excessive amounts of fat in our diets are a major contributor to obesity, high cholesterol levels, coronary heart disease, diabetes and even cancer. Not only is it a fast-track to an unhealthy future – but it can also potentially knock years off our life span.

The universal message we hear again and again is to cut down the amount of fats that we eat, and embark on a healthier, less fatty diet. But what we also need to know is that whilst we need to cut bad fats out of our diet, we do actually need some fats to keep our bodies healthy... good fats.

Good Fats Vs Bad Fats

For the healthy functioning of our bodies, we need certain types of fat in our diet. These particular fats help with digestion and the absorption of vital nutrients, the maintenance of healthy cells & cognitive function, they're beneficial to prostaglandular activity, nerve transmission, immune system function, lowering bad cholesterol and increasing the amount of good cholesterol, (which works to kill off the bad cholesterol!)... to name but a few benefits!

So, the key to balancing fats in our diet is to replace the bad ones with the good ones!

Good Fats

Polyunsaturated Fats

Found in: Oily fish, like salmon, tuna & mackerel. (Omega 3 fatty acids belong to this group.) Sunflower, flaxseed, corn, soybean and safflower oils. Flax seeds & walnuts.

Benefits: Lowers bad cholesterol (LDL cholesterol).

Monounsaturated Fats

Found in: Nuts; pecans, almonds, pistachios, peanuts, walnuts, hazelnuts. Seeds; such as sesame and pumpkin seeds. Avocados, olive oil and canola oil.

Benefits: Lowers bad cholesterol (LDL cholesterol) and increases good cholesterol (HDL cholesterol). Assists weight loss – in particular, body fat.

Bad Fats

Saturated Fats

Found in: Red meat, dairy products, eggs and oils such as palm, palm kernel and coconut.

Risks: Raises bad cholesterol levels in the bloodstream, (LDL).

Trans Fats

Found in: Predominantly found in pre-packaged food, commercially fried foods, fast-food and pre-packaged sugary and savoury snacks.

Risks: Raises bad cholesterol levels (LDL) and lowers good cholesterol levels (HDL). Provokes over-activity of the immune system, causing inflammation associated with stroke, diabetes, heart disease and other chronic conditions.

Tips for Lowering Bad Fats & Increasing Good Fats

Pre-packaged meals

Cut right back on pre-packaged meals and sugary/savoury snacks; not to mention fast-food; which are all generally high in trans fats.

Labels

Always read food labels! Saturated fats will be hard to avoid completely, as they are found in lots of food-stuffs – but you can limit the amount that you eat. Find trans-fat-free alternatives – these fats are a BIG dietary 'no-no'.

Watch out for hydrogenated oils on labels – these are trans fats.

Dairy Products and oils

Use reduced fat dairy products, such as skimmed milk instead of full-fat.

Avoid cooking oils and butters high in saturated or trans fats – opt for polyunsaturated and monounsaturated oils and margarines instead. Use low-fat or fat-free salad dressing.

Meat

Limit the amount of red meat you have in your diet. Trim all visible fat and skins from meat and poultry products. Buy lean cuts of meat.

Fatty acids

Eat oily fish at least 3 times a week – high in Omega 3 fatty acids, these will boost your good cholesterol levels.

Fresh is best

Opt for fresh, unprocessed ingredients where possible – the less food has been 'tampered' with, the healthier and lower in fat it's likely to be.

Fried food

Cut back on fried food – whether it be deep or shallow frying. Grill, steam, microwave or bake where possible. If a recipe requires some frying, use a low-fat polyunsaturated or monounsaturated spray, or cooking oil.

Vegetarian option

Swap a meat-based dinner for a vegetarian option a couple of times a week. Use beans and pulses to bulk up and compensate for a lack of meat.

Snack attack

For snacks, opt for fresh fruits or crudités instead of bad-fat snacks or sweets.

'Low-fat'

Beware products marked as 'low-fat'! They might be lower in fat, but they might not have much nutritional value and who amongst us hasn't been lulled into the false-sense-of-security of having an extra portion... just because it's low-fat...

Of course, a nutritionally balanced and healthy lifestyle is essential to our good health; and the recipes in this book are all geared towards achieving a diet low in the bad fats that cause us ill-health and unwanted weight gain. So get cooking and enjoy!

Low Fat 'Stars' Key for recipes

0 – 2.9g Fat   =   *****

3g – 5.9g Fat   =   ****

6g – 8.9g Fat   =   ***

9.0g – 12.9g Fat   =   **

13g+ Fat   =   *

Banana and Raspberry Bread (12 slices) ****

130g/3/4 cup of fresh raspberries
55ml/1/4 cup of non-fat vanilla yoghurt
2 ripe bananas (mashed)
115g/1 cup of whole wheat flour
115g/1 cup of flour
55ml/1/4 cup of vegetable oil
150g/2/3 cup of sugar
1 egg
1 egg white
1 tbsp baking powder
1/2 tsp bicarbonate of soda
1/2 tsp salt
1 tsp vanilla extract

1. Preheat the oven to 180C/350F/Gas mark 4. Lightly grease or spray a loaf pan with low-fat cooking spray.

2. Place both flours, the baking powder, bicarbonate of soda, salt and sugar in a large bowl and mix together well.

Banana and Raspberry Bread/Cont.

3. Place the egg and egg white in a bowl and lightly beat them together. Add in the mashed banana, vegetable oil, yoghurt and vanilla in a bowl and combine.

4. Add the wet ingredients to the flour mixture and stir in until all the ingredients are moist. Carefully fold in the raspberries.

5. Spoon the mixture into loaf pan and bake in the oven for 50-55 minutes.

Per Serving: 198kcals, 5.5g Fat.

Berry Pancakes (Serves 4) ****

225g/1 cup of frozen mixed berries (thawed & drained)
60g/1/2 cup of flour
60g/1/2 cup of whole wheat flour
280ml/1 1/4 cups of low-fat buttermilk
3 tbsp sugar
1 tsp baking powder
1/2 tsp bicarbonate of soda
1/4 tsp salt
1 egg (lightly beaten)
2 tsp vegetable oil
1 tsp vanilla extract

1. Place all of the dry ingredients in a bowl and mix together well.

2. Place the buttermilk, egg, vanilla and oil in a separate bowl and mix together well. Add in the wet ingredients and combine. Carefully fold in the berries until evenly distributed.

3. Spray a non-stick frying pan with fat-free cooking spray and heat on a medium/high heat. Pour in 1/4 cup of batter and swirl around the pan to cover as much of the base as possible.

As the edges cook and begin to puff, use a spatula to lift the edges of the pancake.

4. Flip over the pancake after about a further minute of cooking and cook the reverse side until golden brown (1-2 minutes).

5. Serve with more berries, (if desired), and a dollop of low-fat vanilla yoghurt.

Per Serving: 240kcals, 5g Fat.

Cheese, Ham and Spinach Strata (Serves 4) ****

3 slices lean cooked ham (chopped)
150g day-old French bread (cubed)
150g of frozen spinach (thawed, chopped and squeezed dry)
225ml/1 cup of skimmed milk
1 egg
2 egg whites
110g/1/2 cup low-fat grated cheddar cheese
1 tsp Dijon mustard
Black pepper (to season)

1. Preheat oven to 180/350F/Gas mark 4. Lightly grease a baking dish or spray with low-fat cooking spray.

2. Place the egg and egg whites in a bowl and whisk together. Add in half the cheese, the milk, mustard, ham and spinach and mix together well.

3. Add in the bread cubes and coat well with the mixture. Pour all of the mixture into the baking dish and top with the remaining cheese and some black pepper, (according to taste).

4. Place in the oven and cook for 35-40 minutes.

Per Serving: 203kcals, 5.8g Fat.

Crunchy French Toast (Serves 4) *****

160g/4 cups of cornflakes (crushed)
2 tbsp orange juice
4 slices wholemeal bread
2 tbsp skimmed milk
2 egg whites

1. Spray a non-stick frying pan with low-fat cooking spray and place over a low heat.

2. Place the crushed cornflakes in a large bowl.

3. Place the orange juice, milk and egg whites in a separate bowl and beat together well.

4. Dip the bread slices into the mixture, covering both sides and then coat each slice with the crushed cornflakes.

5. Add to the frying pan and cook until both sides are golden brown, (turning them whilst cooking).

Per Serving: 194kcals, 1g Fat.

Light French Toast & Banana (Serves 8) ****

16 slices wholemeal bread
4 egg whites
2 bananas (mashed)
225ml/1 cup of skimmed milk
1 tsp sweetener
1 tsp ground cinnamon
1 tbsp low-fat butter

1. Place the skimmed milk, mashed banana, cinnamon, egg whites and sweetener in a bowl and whisk together.

2. Dip the bread slices into the mixture, covering both sides.

3. Spray a non-stick frying pan with low-fat cooking spray and add the low fat butter. Place over a medium heat and melt the butter. Add the bread slices and cook until golden brown both sides, (turn whilst cooking).

Per Serving (2 slices): 233kcals, 4g Fat.

Scrambled Eggs & Smoked Salmon (Serves 4) ****

4 eggs
8 egg whites
Black pepper (to season)
50g smoked salmon (cut into thin strips)
Fresh dill, or chopped chives

1. Place the eggs and egg whites in a bowl and whisk together. Add black pepper to season, according to taste. Spray a large non-stick frying pan with low-fat cooking spray and heat over a low/medium heat. Add the eggs and gently cook them until curds begin to form.

2. Using a spatula or a wooden spoon, move the eggs around so that the uncooked parts cook. Keep doing this for 1-2 minutes until the eggs are almost set. Stir in the salmon and mix in well. Remove from the heat and serve with a slice of whole wheat toast.

Per Serving: 119kcals, 5.6g Fat.

Simply Pancakes (Makes 10-12) *****

115g/1 cup of flour
1/2 tsp salt
2 eggs (lightly beaten)
280ml/11/4 cup of skimmed milk

1. Place the flour and salt in a bowl and mix together well. Make a well in the centre of the flour and add in the eggs.

2. Whisk the egg and flour together, whilst pouring in the milk, a little at a time. Mix well, making sure that the mixture is smooth. Stand for 3-5 minutes.

3. Spray a non-stick frying pan with fat-free cooking spray and heat on a medium/high heat. Pour in 1/4 cup of batter and swirl around the pan to cover as much of the base as possible. As the edges cook and begin to puff, use a spatula to lift the edges of the pancake.

4. Flip over the pancake after about a further minute of cooking and cook the reverse side until golden brown (1-2 minutes).

5. Serve each pancake with a topping of your choice. Fruit is a good low-fat option.

Per Pancake: 57kcals, 1g Fat.

Strawberry Breakfast Drink (Serves 2) *****

110g/1/2 cup of strawberries
150ml/2/3 cup of low-fat natural yoghurt
150ml/2/3 cup of skimmed milk

Place all the ingredients into a blender and blend until smooth. Serve in 2 tall glasses.

Per Serving: 77kcals, 0.8g Fat.

Strawberry Yogurt Granola (Makes 4) ****

1 banana (sliced)
225g/2 cup of small strawberries (halved)
225g/1 cup low-fat strawberry yoghurt
230g/2 cups of low-fat granola
2 strawberries (sliced)

1. In 4 glass dessert bowls, alternate a layer of strawberries, yoghurt, granola and then banana, (repeat until filled).

2. Sprinkle the top with a little of the granola and a couple of slices of strawberry.

Per Serving: 400kcals, 5.1g Fat.

Tropical Fruit Smoothie (Serves 4) *****

2 kiwifruit
1 mango (chopped)
2 frozen bananas (sliced)
225g/1 cup of canned crushed pineapple
Juice of 1 large orange
225ml/1 cup of low-fat buttermilk

Place all the ingredients in a blender and blend until smooth. Serve in tall glasses with ice-cubes.

Low Fat 'Stars' Key for recipes

0 – 2.9g Fat	=	*****
3g – 5.9g Fat	=	****
6g – 8.9g Fat	=	***
9.0g – 12.9g Fat	=	**
13g+ Fat	=	*

Chicken Caesar Salad (Serves 4) ****

Salad:

4 cooked chicken breasts (skinless & chopped)
1 head of romaine lettuce (torn)
1/4 cup fresh Parmesan cheese (grated)
1 cup of low-fat croutons
Fresh ground black pepper (to season)

Dressing:

1 clove of garlic (crushed)
1 tsp Dijon mustard
75g/1/3 cup of non-fat plain yoghurt (drained)
2 tbsp fresh lemon juice
1 tsp olive oil
1 tsp white wine vinegar
1 tsp Worcestershire sauce
1 tsp anchovy paste

1. Place the romaine lettuce in a large serving bowl.

2. Place the dressing ingredients in a bowl and whisk together.

3. Top the romaine lettuce with the chicken, croutons and sprinkle over with the parmesan cheese.

Chicken Caesar Salad/Cont.

4. Drizzle the dressing over the salad and gently toss; coating all the ingredients.

5. Season with black pepper, if desired.

Per Serving: 188kcals, 4.5g Fat.

Chicken Nuggets (Serves 8) *****

8 chicken breasts (skinless)
55g/1/2 cup of flour
80g/2 cups of cornflakes (crushed)
1/2 tsp black pepper
1/2 tsp paprika
2 egg whites
110ml/1/2 cup of low fat buttermilk

1. Preheat the oven to 230C/450F/Gas mark 8. Spray a baking tray with low-fat cooking spray.

2. Place the flour, black pepper and paprika in a bowl and mix together.

3. In a separate bowl, place the eggs and buttermilk mix together well. In a third bowl, place the crushed cornflakes.

4. Cut the chicken breasts into approximately 11/2 inch pieces and roll in the flour mixture.

5. Removing them one at a time, shake off any excess flour and dip them in the milk/egg mixture. Finally, coat each nugget by rolling them in the crushed cornflakes.

6. Place the nuggets on the baking tray and cook in the oven for 10-12 minutes, turning them half way through.

Per Serving: 182kcals, 1.6g Fat.

Chunky Chicken and Vegetable Soup (Serves 8-10) ****

1 small uncooked chicken (skinned)
1 onion (chopped)
1-2 cloves of garlic (crushed)
2 carrots (sliced)
1 stalk of celery (sliced)
2 quarts/2 litres of water
1 courgette (sliced)
1/2 small head of cabbage (chopped)
300g/1 & 1/3 canned kidney beans (drained)
1 sweet potato (peeled and diced)
1 tsp salt
1/2 tsp black pepper

1. Place the onion, garlic and chicken in a large saucepan and cover with water. Place over a medium/high heat and bring to the boil. Reduce the heat and leave to simmer for 55-60 minutes.

2. Remove the chicken from the saucepan and put to one side to cool a little for 5-10 minutes.

3. Skim any fat from the surface of the chicken broth. Remove the chicken meat from the bones and place back in the saucepan.

4. Add the remaining ingredients to the saucepan and return to the boil. Reduce the heat and leave to simmer for 20-25 minutes.

Per Serving: 108kcal, 3g Fat.

Curried Chicken Salad (Serves 4) ***

4 cooked chicken breasts (skinless)
450g/1 lb baby spinach
2 celery stalks (chopped)
1 apple (chopped)
40g/1/4 cup of raisins
20g/1/4 cup of almonds (sliced)
80g/1/3 cup plain low-fat yoghurt
60ml/1/4 cup fat-free mayonnaise
2 tsp curry powder
1 tbsp chopped coriander

1. Place the mayonnaise, curry powder and yoghurt in a bowl and mix together well.

2. In a separate bowl, place the chicken, almonds, apple, raisins and celery. Add the dressing and gently toss, coating all the ingredients. Top with coriander.

3. Evenly distribute the baby spinach over 8 serving plates and top with the chicken salad.

Per Serving: 227kcals, 6.6g Fat.

Ham and Turkey Wrap (Makes 2) ****

4 thin slices of low-fat honey ham
4 thin slices of low-fat turkey breast
3-4 tsp Dijon mustard (or fat-free mayonnaise)
2/3 leaves of romaine lettuce (shredded)
2 6-inch whole-wheat tortilla wraps

1. Spread the Dijon mustard, (or mayonnaise), on the wraps.

2. Spread the romaine lettuce over the top and lay on 2 of each of the slices of meat. Roll the wraps and cut in half. Serve with a salad garnish and cherry tomatoes.

Per Wrap: 198kcals, 3.3g Fat.

Lemon & Yoghurt Chicken Salad Wraps (Serves 4) *****

2 tbsp fat-free mayonnaise

3 tbsp low-fat yoghurt

1 tsp lemon juice

3 chicken breasts (cooked and chopped)

1 red pepper

1 green pepper

225ml/1 cup of canned sweetcorn (drained)

225ml/1 cup of canned black beans (drained)

1 red onion

1/2 cucumber

1 tomato

1 iceberg lettuce

1. Finely chop the peppers, onion, cucumber and tomato and put to one side.

2. Place the fat-free mayonnaise, lemon juice and yoghurt in a bowl and mix well.

3. Place the chopped chicken breast, the chopped peppers, onion, cucumber and tomato; and finally the black beans and sweetcorn. Add in the dressing and mix well.

4. Arrange the lettuce leaves in a large dish and cover with the chicken salad. Serve with 4 wholewheat tortillas, to make individual wraps.

Per serving: 166kcals, 1.9g Fat.

Lentil and Tuna Salad (Serves 8) **

370g canned tuna (drained & flaked)
750g canned lentils (drained)
4 tomatoes (finely chopped)
2 small red onions (finely chopped)
1 tsp ground coriander
1 egg (hard boiled)
5 tbsp virgin olive oil
2 tbsp lemon juice
2 tsp wholegrain mustard
1 tsp cumin
2 cloves of garlic
2 tbsp chopped coriander
Black pepper (to season)

1. Place the lemon juice, garlic, mustard, oil, cumin and coriander in a bowl and whisk together.

2. Place the tomatoes, egg, onion and lentils in a large bowl and mix together. Stir in the flaked tuna, followed by the chopped coriander.

3. Pour the dressing over the salad and mix together well. Season with black pepper, according to taste.

Per Serving: 227kcals, 9g Fat.

Savoury Cheese, Ham & Celery Grills (Serves 4) ***

6 tbsp low-fat natural yoghurt
12 thin slices of lean ham
1 bunch spring onions (finely chopped)
4 sticks of celery (sliced into 3 equal portions = 12 total)
4 tbsp low-fat Parmesan cheese (grated)
170g/3/4 cup of low-fat soft cheese
Salt and pepper (to season)

1. Place the ham flat and place one portion of celery in the centre of each. Roll the ham around the celery to create a wrapped effect. Place 3 ham/celery wraps in the bottom of a heatproof serving dish, (x4).

2. Evenly sprinkle the chopped spring onions over the ham and celery rolls and season with salt and pepper, according to taste. Place the soft cheese and yoghurt in a bowl and mix then spoon over the ham and celery rolls.

3. Place under a medium grill for 3 minutes. Remove from the grill and sprinkle over with 1 tbsp parmesan cheese, per serving. Place back under the grill for a further 3-4 minutes. Serve with a tomato salad.

Per Serving: 155kcals, 6.9g Fat.

Shrimp and Sweet-Mango Salad (Serves 8) *****

675g cooked shrimp
1 romaine lettuce
2 mangos (peeled & cubed)
110g/1/2 cup of spring onions (finely sliced)
8 vine-ripe tomatoes (cut into wedges)
2 tsp jalapeno pepper (minced)
1 1/2 tbsp brown sugar
Juice of 1 lime
1 1/2 tbsp soy sauce
1 1/2 tbsp fish sauce
4 tbsp water

1. Place mango, spring onions and shrimp in a bowl. Place the soy and fish sauces, jalapeno pepper, sugar and lime juice in a jug and whisk together.

Shrimp and Sweet-Mango Salad/Cont.

2. Pour over the shrimp mixture and toss well. Cover and place in the refrigerator for 15 minutes.

3. Divide the romaine lettuce amongst 8 serving bowls/plates. Remove the salad from the fridge and divide equally on top of the lettuce. Garnish with the tomato wedges and serve immediately.

Per Serving: 150kcals, 1.9g Fat.

Skewered Chicken (Serves 4) ****

500g chicken breasts (skinless & chopped into 1 inch pieces)
225g/1 cup of cherry tomatoes
3 tbsp tomato puree
1 tbsp fresh rosemary (chopped)
2 tbsp clear honey
2 tbsp Worcestershire sauce
8 skewers (if wooden, pre-soak for 30 minutes)

1. Preheat the grill to a medium heat. Place the honey, Worcestershire sauce, tomato puree and rosemary in a bowl and mix together. Add the cubed chicken and stir well, coating the chicken pieces evenly.

2. Divide the chicken equally and thread the chicken onto 8 skewers. Cover with any of the remaining sauce. Place under the grill and cook for 8-10 minutes, turning occasionally.

3. Serve with a mixed salad, or alternatively a bed of freshly cooked couscous or rice.

Per Serving (2 skewers):
195kcals, 4g Fat.

Southern-Style Chicken Salad (Serves 8) *****

8 cooked chicken breasts (skinless & cubed)
600g/4 cups of baby spinach
2 tomatoes (chopped)
1/2 red onion (finely chopped)
110g/1/2 cup of sweet corn
1 red pepper (chopped)
110g/1/2 cup of fat-free mayonnaise
110g/1/2 cup of pain, non-fat yoghurt
1 tsp lime juice
225g/1 cup of canned black beans (drained & washed)
1 1/2 tsp cumin

1. Place the yoghurt, cumin, mayonnaise and lime juice in a bowl and mix together well.

2. In a separate bowl, place the chicken, black beans, sweet corn, tomato, pepper and onion. Add the dressing and gently toss, coating all the ingredients.

3. Evenly distribute the baby spinach over 8 serving plates and top with the chicken salad.

Per Serving: 166kcals, 1.9g Fat.

Thai-Style Chicken Salad (Serves 4) **

8 romaine lettuce leaves
4 cooked chicken breasts (skinless & chopped)
55g/1/4 cup of smooth peanut butter (softened)
450g/2 cups of shredded coleslaw mix (dry)
4 tbsp rice vinegar
2 tbsp soy sauce
3 large tomatoes (sliced)
Juice of 1/2 lime
1/2 tsp ginger (minced)

1. Place the soy sauce, peanut butter, lime juice, ginger and rice vinegar in a bowl and combine well. Stir in the chicken, coating it well.

Thai-Style Chicken Salad/Cont.

2. Place the coleslaw in a bowl and drizzle with the rice. Toss well to coat the coleslaw.

3. Place two lettuce leaves on each serving plate. Divide the coleslaw mix equally amongst the plates and garnish around the edges of the lettuce with slices of tomato.

4. Top the plates with equal amount of the chicken mixture and serve immediately.

Per Serving: 234kcals, 10.5g Fat.

Spicy Burgers with Yoghurt & Mint Dressing (Serves 8) ***

675g/1 1/2 lb lean minced beef
2 egg whites
8 whole wheat pitta pockets
1 cucumber (sliced)
1 clove of garlic (crushed)
75g/3/4 cup of onion (finely chopped)
110ml/1/2 cup of tomato puree
335g/1 1/2 cups of low-fat plain yoghurt
1 tbsp fresh mint (finely chopped)
8 tomatoes (sliced)
1 tsp cumin
1 tsp paprika
1/2 tsp tumeric
1/2 tsp cardamon
Ground black pepper (to season)

1. Place the yoghurt and chopped mint in a small bowl and mix together well. Cover and place in the refrigerator.

2. Place the minced beef, egg whites, onion, tomato puree, spices and seasoning in a large mixing bowl and combine together gently with a fork.

3. Once combined, form 8 individual 'patties' from the mixture. Place the patties under a medium heat grill and cook for approximately 5 minutes, per side.

4. Warm the pitta breads, as per the packet instructions and cut in half. Place a burger in each of the pitta pockets and fill with the sliced tomatoes and cucumber.

5. Remove the yoghurt dressing from the refrigerator and add to the pitta pockets, according to taste.

Per Serving: 268kcals, 6.2g Fat.

Tuna and Spinach Salad (Serves 4-6) ****

800g/14oz tinned tuna chunks
900g/6 cups of fresh baby spinach (washed & dried)
100g/1 cup of canned white beans (rinsed & drained)
425g/15oz canned artichoke hearts (drained & halved)
100g/1 cup of sliced mushrooms
2 tbsp lemon juice
2 tbsp water
2 tbsp white wine vinegar
1 tbsp extra virgin olive oil

1. Place the oil, lemon juice, vinegar and water in a jug and whisk.

2. Place the spinach leaves in a large bowl and add in the white beans, tomatoes, mushrooms, tuna and artichoke hearts.

3. Drizzle the dressing the over the salad and toss well.

Serve in individual serving bowls.

Per Serving: 203kcals, 3.4g Fat.

Chicken Pizza (Serves 4-6) ***

225g/1 cup of shredded cooked chicken
300g pre-baked whole wheat pizza base
225g/1 cup of low-fat cheese
110g/1/2 cup of tomato puree
1 clove of garlic (crushed)
110g/1/2 can of artichoke hearts (halved)
110g/1/2 cup of black olives (sliced)
220g jar of roasted red peppers (chopped)
1/2 tsp oregano
1/2 tsp basil

1. Preheat the oven to 230C/450F/Gas mark 8. Spread the tomato puree evenly over the pizza base.

2. Sprinkle the vegetable toppings and chicken over the pizza and top with the cheese.

3. Place directly onto the middle shelf of the oven and bake for 10-12 minutes.

Per Serving, (6 slices): 230kcals, 6.4g Fat.

Low Fat 'Stars' Key for recipes

0 – 2.9g Fat	=	*****
3g – 5.9g Fat	=	****
6g – 8.9g Fat	=	***
9.0g – 12.9g Fat	=	**
13g+ Fat	=	*

Couscous Salad (Serves 6) ****

450ml/2 cups of cooked whole wheat couscous
225ml/1 cup of canned chickpeas (drained)
Juice of 2 lemons
150g/1 cup of cucumber (chopped)
1/2 red onion (finely chopped)
200g/1 cup of tomatoes (chopped)
1 tbsp olive oil
1/3 cup of fresh mint

1. Place the lemon juice and olive oil and whisk together.

2. In a separate bowl place the couscous, tomato, onion, chickpeas, cucumber and mint.

3. Pour the dressing over the salad and gently toss, coating all the ingredients.

Cover and place in the refrigerator for 2-3 hours.

Per Serving: 162kcals, 3.2g Fat.

Courgette and Mushroom Frittata (Serves 4) ****

1 courgette (halved, lengthwise and sliced)
55g/1/4 cup of low-fat soft cheese
170g/3/4 cup of mushrooms (sliced)
55ml/1/4 cup of skimmed milk
2 eggs
4 egg whites
1/2 tsp oregano
Black pepper (to season)

1. Spray a non-stick frying pan, (with a heat resistant handle), with low-fat cooking spray and heat over a medium heat.

2. Add the courgettes and mushrooms and sauté for approximately 4 minutes.

3. Preheat the grill to a medium heat.

4. Place the eggs, egg whites, black pepper, milk and oregano in a bowl and whisk together.

5. Pour over the vegetables in the frying pan and sprinkle with the cheese.

6. Cook for about 4-5 minutes on a low heat and then transfer to the grill. Cook for a further 3-4 minutes, until the eggs are set and the top is golden brown.

7. Remove from the grill – remembering that the handle will be red-hot. Cut into 4 slices and serve immediately with a side salad.

Per Serving: 85kcals, 4g Fat.

Minestrone Soup (Serves 4-6) *****

620ml/2 3/4 cups of vegetable broth
335ml/1 1/2 cups of water
110g/1/2 cup of chopped onion
2 cloves of garlic (crushed)
150g tomato puree
1 tsp Italian seasoning
1/2 tsp black pepper
450g/2 cups of canned mixed vegetables (drained)
55g/1/2 cup of elbow macaroni
1 tbsp olive oil

1. Place the olive oil in a large non-stick saucepan and heat; add in the garlic and onion and sauté for 3-4 minutes, until tender.

2. Add the water, tomato puree, broth and seasonings and bring to the boil; stirring well. Reduce the heat and simmer for 10 minutes.

3. Add in the macaroni and mixed vegetables and cook for a further 10 minutes, (or as per macaroni cooking instructions). Remove from the heat and serve.

4. Sprinkle with low-fat parmesan cheese, if desired.

Per Serving: 99kcals, 2g Fat.

Scalloped Tomatoes (Serves 4-6) ****

4-5 tomatoes (sliced)
100g/2 cups of white bread cubes
50g/1/2 cup of low-fat grated cheese
1 onion (chopped)
2 tsp olive oil
1/2 tsp salt
4 tsp brown sugar
1/2 tsp dried basil
Black pepper (to season)

1. Preheat the oven to 190C/375F/Gas mark 5. Heat the olive oil in a non-stick saucepan and add the onion. Sauté for 3-4 minutes.

2. Add the pepper, basil, salt, brown sugar and tomatoes to the saucepan and stir. Add in the bread cubes and stir all the ingredients together well.

3. Pour the mixture into a lightly greased casserole dish and place in the oven for 30 minutes. Top with grated cheese and return to the oven for 5 minutes. Remove from the oven and serve with a green salad and crusty rolls.

Per Serving: 120kcals, 4g Fat.

Spinach and Apple Salad (Serves 6) *****

150g/1 cup of fresh baby spinach
2 small apples (thinly chopped)
50g/1/2 cup of red onion (thinly sliced)
2 tbsp fresh lime juice
2 tbsp fresh orange juice
2 tsp clear honey
2 tsp Dijon mustard
1/4 tsp salt
1/4 tsp black pepper
25g/1/4 cup of reduced-fat blue cheese (crumbled)

1. Place the mustard, juices, salt, pepper and honey in a bowl and mix together.

2. Place the sliced onions, chopped apple and spinach in a large bowl and add the dressing, coating all the contents well.

3. Top with the crumbled blue cheese and serve.

Per Serving: 60kcals, 2g Fat.

Spinach and Herb Omelet (Serves 1) *****

120g/3/4 cup of fresh baby spinach (chopped)
3 egg whites
1 tbsp skimmed milk
1/2 tsp mixed herbs
1/4 tsp black pepper
1 tbsp low-fat grated cheddar
1 green pepper
1 red pepper
1 tomato

1. Place the egg whites, herbs and milk in a bowl and combine well.

2. Lightly oil or spray a non-stick frying pan with low-fat cooking spray and heat over a medium/high heat. Add in the spinach and cook for 1-2 minutes.

3. As the spinach begins to 'wilt' pour the egg white mixture over it, tilting the pan to cover the whole base of the pan. Allow the mixture to set around the edges, lifting them carefully with a spatula and running any remaining liquid to the edges.

4. Cook until the eggs are set and sprinkle the cheese over the top. Fold the omelet in half and cook for another 30 seconds. Serve with tomato and sliced peppers.

Per Serving: 81kcals, 1.6g Fat.

Sweet Potato Hash (Serves 4-6) ****

600g/4 cups of peeled & diced sweet potatoes
350g/2 cups of diced courgettes
225g/1 1/2 cups of diced red onions
2 cloves of garlic (crushed)
1 red pepper (chopped)
1 red pepper (chopped)
1 green pepper (chopped)
1/2 tbsp vegetable oil
225g/1 cup of sweetcorn
75g/1/2 cup of spring onions (thinly sliced)
55g/1/4 cup of jalapeno peppers (seeded & chopped)
55g/1/4 cup of chopped parsley
1 tsp ground cumin
1 tsp chili powder
1/2 tsp salt
1/4 tsp black pepper

1. Place the vegetable oil in a non-stick frying pan and heat until warm. Add the sweet potatoes and sauté for 5-6 minutes. Add in the onion and sauté for a further 4-5 minutes.

2. Add in the sweetcorn, red and green peppers, courgettes and jalapenos; sauté for another 5-6 minutes, stirring frequently.

3. Add in the garlic and spring onions and continue to sauté for 4-5 minutes.

4. Add in the parsley, spices and seasoning and mix well. Cook for a further 2-3 minutes.

Per Serving: 196kcals, 4g Fat.

Three-Bean Enchiladas (Serves 8) *

200g/1 cup of dried kidney beans
200g/1 cup of dried pinto beans
200g/1 cup of dried navy beans
2 cloves of garlic (crushed)
150g/1 cup of chopped onion
2 tsps chili powder
225g/1 cup of grated low-fat cheese (optional)
1 1/2 tsp ground cumin
225ml/1 cup of enchilada sauce
110g/1/2 cup of canned green chilies (chopped, undrained)
3/4 tsp salt
16 corn tortillas (2 each = 1 serving)
2.7 ltr/12 cups of water
2 tbsp olive oil (to oil baking dish)

1. Preheat the oven to 180C/350F/Gas mark 4. Wash the beans thoroughly and place in a pan. Cover the beans with cold water, (2 inches above the beans) and place a lid on the pan.

2. Place over a medium/high heat and bring to the boil; simmer for 2-3 minutes. Remove from the heat and leave to stand for 1 hour.

3. Drain the beans and return to the pan. Add 12 cups of water and the salt. Place over a medium/high heat and bring back to the boil. Cover the pan and simmer for 1 hour, (or until the beans are cooked and tender).

4. Drain the beans, reserving 1/2 cup of the liquid. Place the drained beans in a food processor, with the onion, garlic, chili powder, cumin and green chilies. Process the ingredients for 5-10 seconds – until the mixture is thick and chunky.

5. Brush each of the tortillas with water and equally divide the bean mixture among the tortillas, (placing the mixture in a strip down the centre of each, so that each can be 'wrapped').

6. Roll each of the tortillas up and place in a lightly oiled baking dish, (you may need 2 dishes), with the seam-side of the tortilla facing down.

Three-Bean Enchiladas/Cont.

7. Pour the enchilada sauce equally over the tortillas. Cover the baking dish and place in the oven for 20 minutes.

8. Remove from the oven and top with the low-fat cheese, (if desired). Return to the oven uncovered and bake for a further 5 minutes.

Per serving: 354kcals, Total Fat 19.6g.

Spicy Courgette Soup (Serves 4) ****

2 courgettes (cut into 11/2 inch slices)
4 tbsps cooked rice
2 cloves of garlic (crushed)
1/2 tsp cumin
2 tbsps mild chilli powder
1.5 litres/6 3/4 cups of vegetable stock
Salt & pepper (to season)
Lime wedges (to serve)
2 tbsps vegetable oil

1. Heat the oil in a saucepan and add the garlic. Cook for 2-3 minutes, add the cumin and chilli powder and cook for a further 1 minute.

2. Add the vegetable stock, rice and courgettes and bring to the boil. Reduce the heat and simmer gently for 10 minutes, (until the courgettes are just tender). Season according to taste.

3. Serve immediately, with lime wedges to squeeze into the soup, if desired.

Per Serving: 213kcal, 3.4g Fat.

Fruity Couscous (Serves 4) ****

150ml/1 & 1/3 cup of quick-cook couscous
1/2 orange (segmented)
225ml/1 cup of orange juice
90g/1/2 cup of red grapes (halved)
1/2 tbsp low-fat margarine
1/2 tsp orange peel (grated)
40g/1/4 cup of golden raisins
1/4 tsp salt
75ml/1/3 cup of firm tofu (drained & cubed)

1. Place the margarine, grated orange peel, orange juice and salt in a saucepan and bring to the boil.

2. Add in the couscous and stir in well. Remove from the heat and cover the pan. Leave to stand for 5 minutes, (check packet instructions to ensure standing time is the same).

3. Fluff the couscous with a fork and stir in the remaining ingredients. Mix together well. Serve either still warm, or cold.

Per Serving: 247kcal, 3g Fat.

Vegetable Stir-Fry (Serves 4) ****

55ml/1/4 cup of clear honey
55ml/1/4 cup of soy sauce (or preferred stir-fry sauce)
1/4 tsp red pepper flakes (crushed)
3 tbsps olive oil
350g/2 cups of broccoli florets
150g/2 cups of mushrooms (sliced)
200g/2 cups of bean sprouts
1 onion (chopped)
1 carrot (cut diagonally into 1/2 inch slices)

1. Place the honey, sauce and pepper flakes in a bowl and mix well. Place to one side. Place the olive oil in a wok and heat on a medium heat.

2. Add the vegetables and toss whilst cooking for 2 minutes. Add in the bean sprouts and cook for 1 minute.

3. Add in the honey sauce and coat all the vegetables. Cook for a further 1-2 minutes.

Serve with either noodles or rice.

Per serving: 157kcal, 5g Fat.

Black Bean and Rice Salad (Serves 4) ****

425g canned black beans (drained & rinsed)
1 jalapeno pepper (finely chopped)
230g/2 cups of brown rice (cooked)
225g/1 cup of canned sweet corn (drained)
1 tbsp chili powder
2 tsp cumin
1/4 cup of fresh coriander (chopped)
Juice of 1 lemon
1 tbsp olive oil

1. Place the olive oil, lemon, chili powder and cumin in a small bowl and mix together.

2. Place the rice, chopped jalapeno, coriander and black beans in a mixing bowl and combine well.

3. Pour the dressing over the rice salad and toss well.

Per Serving: 270kcals, 5g Fat.

Tomato and White Bean Soup (Serves 6) *****

900ml/4 cups of vegetable broth
300g/2 cups of canned white navy beans
375g/1 & 2/3 cup of canned chopped tomatoes
2 carrots (sliced)
2 sticks of celery (sliced)
1 onion (chopped)
1 tsp oregano
1 tbsp olive oil
Grated Parmesan cheese (optional)

1. Heat the olive oil in a large saucepan and add the carrots, celery and onions. Sauté for 5-6 minutes, stirring frequently. Add the herbs and cook for 3 minutes.

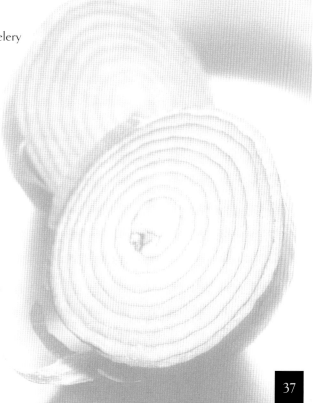

2. Add in the broth and chopped tomatoes and bring to the boil. Reduce the heat, add in the white beans and simmer for 20 minutes.

Serve immediately and sprinkle with Parmesan cheese, if desired.

Per Serving, (without Parmesan cheese): 173kcals, 2.2g Fat.

Veggie-Chilli Stuffed Potatoes (Serves 8) ****

8 jacket potatoes
850g canned vegetarian chili
2 small onions (chopped)
2 garlic cloves (crushed)
2 tsps ground cumin
1/4 tsp salt
450g grated low-fat cheddar cheese (optional)
2 tsps olive oil
225g fat-free soured cream
Dash of balsamic vinegar
Chives (to garnish)
1 tsp pepper.

1. Prick and cook the potatoes in the oven, (as per jacket potato cooking methods), according to their weight.

2. 20 minutes before the potatoes are ready, place the olive oil in a frying pan and add in the chopped onion; sauté for 3-4 minutes.

3. Add in the chili, salt, cumin, garlic and a dash of vinegar, mix well and simmer for 15 minutes.

4. Remove the potatoes from the oven and slit to open. Mash the potato slightly to soften and spoon some of the chili mix over each potato.

5. Add a spoonful of soured cream and top with grated cheese and chopped chives, if desired.

Sprinkle with pepper.

Per Serving: 293kcals, 5g fat.

Low Fat 'Stars' Key for recipes

0 – 2.9g Fat	=	*****
3g – 5.9g Fat	=	****
6g – 8.9g Fat	=	***
9.0g – 12.9g Fat	=	**
13g+ Fat	=	*

Baked Chicken & Wedges; Southern-Style! (Serves 4) ***

8 chicken drumsticks (skinless)
4 baking potatoes (approx. 225g each)
1 tbsp sunflower oil
2 tbsps plain flour
6 tbsps dry white breadcrumbs
1 egg (beaten)
1/2 tsp paprika
1/8 tsp cayenne pepper
2 tsps coarse sea-salt
1/2 tsp thyme
2 tbsp cold water
Salt & pepper (to season)

Potato Wedges:

1. Preheat the oven to 200C/400F/Gas mark 6. Wash and scrub the potatoes, (do not peel), and cut each into 8 equal sized wedges. Place the oil in a bowl and coat each of the wedges.

2. Place the wedges on a non-stick baking sheet, (skin side down). Sprinkle over the sea salt and leave to one side.

Chicken Drumsticks:

3. Place the beaten egg and water in a bowl and mix . Leave to one side.

Baked Chicken & Wedges; Southern-Style!/Cont.

4. Place the breadcrumbs in a separate bowl and leave to one side.

5. Place the spices, thyme, seasoning and flour in a bowl and mix together.

6. Coat each of the chicken drumsticks with the flour mixture, then dip each into the egg, followed by the breadcrumbs. Transfer straight onto a non-stick baking sheet.

7. Place in the oven, alongside the potato wedges, for 30 minutes. Cook the wedges until they are golden brown and turn the chicken drumsticks halfway through the cooking time.

8. Remove from the oven when ready and turn out the potato wedges onto kitchen towel, to absorb any excess fat. Serve with a side salad.

Per Serving: 402kcals, 7.4g Fat.

Beef and Squash Slow-Cook Stew (Serves 8) ****

450g lean stewing beef (trimmed)
1 butternut squash
225g/1 cup of Portabello mushrooms (sliced)
1 onion (sliced)
450g/2 cups of canned crushed tomatoes
75g/1/3 cup of baby carrots (whole)
2 tsp Worcestershire sauce
1 tsp thyme
1 tsp oregano
Black pepper (to season)

1. Peel the butternut squash and cut into 1 1/2 inch pieces. Spray a non-stick frying pan with cooking spray and place over a medium heat.

2. Add the stewing beef and cook for 2-3 minutes, until browned. Remove from the heat and put to one side.

3. Place the beef and vegetables in a 3.5 litre crockpot. Add the tomatoes, oregano, thyme, Worcestershire sauce and black pepper. Cook on a low heat for 6-8 hours.

Per Serving: 288kcals, 4.9g Fat.

Beef & Three-Bean Slow-Cook Chilli (Serves 4) ****

175g lean minced beef
100g/1 cup of canned kidney beans (drained & rinsed)
100g/1 cup of canned pinto beans (drained & rinsed)
100g/1 cup of canned black beans (drained & rinsed)
55g/1/4 cup of jalapeno peppers (sliced)
375g/1 & 2/3 cups of canned crushed tomatoes
1 small onion (chopped)
1 carrot (diced)
1/2 tbsp chilli powder
1 tsp cumin powder

1. Preheat the oven to 160C/325F/Gas mark 3. Spray the inside of a 3 litre crockpot with low-fat cooking spray.

Beef & Three-Bean Slow-Cook Chilli/Cont.

2. Place the onions and carrots at the bottom of the crockpot.

3. Spray a non-stick frying pan with low-fat cooking spray and place over a medium heat. Add in the minced beef and cook until browned. Sprinkle over with the cumin and chilli powder.

4. Drain any fat from the beef and spoon into the crockpot. Add in the 3 beans, crushed tomatoes and jalapeno peppers. Cover and cook on a low heat for 6-8 hours.

Per Serving: **263kcals, 3.4g Fat.**

Curried Chicken and Apple Salad (Serves 8) *****

8 cooked chicken breasts (skinless & cubed)
2 stalks of celery (sliced)
2 apples (unpeeled & diced)
2 tsp curry powder
75g/1/2 cup of raisins
1 1/2 tbsp lemon juice
110g/1/2 cup of low-fat yoghurt
110g/1/2 cup of fat-free mayonnaise

1. Place the diced chicken, apple, raisins and celery in a bowl and mix together well.

2. Place the yoghurt, lemon juice, curry powder and mayonnaise in a bowl and whisk. Pour over the chicken salad and toss well to coat.

Serve in individual serving bowls.

Per Serving: **229kcal, 2.6g Fat.**

Chicken and Asparagus Soup (Serves 8) *****

250g/2 cups of fresh asparagus
1800ml/8 cups of chicken stock
300ml/1 & 1/3 cup of dry white wine
1 sprig of parsley
1/2 tsp tarragon
1/2 tsp dill
1 clove of garlic (crushed)
75g/1 cup of vermicelli rice noodles
1 leek (washed & shredded)
700g lean cooked chicken (finely shredded)
Salt and black pepper, to season

1. Wash the asparagus and trim away the ends. Cut each spear into pieces approx. 11/2 inch long. Keep to one side.

2. Pour the wine and chicken stock into a large saucepan and heat over a medium/high heat. Bring to the boil and then reduce heat; simmer gently.

3. Add the garlic, herbs, asparagus and noodles. Cover the pan and simmer for 5-6 minutes.

4. Add in the shredded chicken and salt and pepper, to season. Simmer for a further 4-5 minutes.

5. Remove the sprig of parsley from the soup and discard. Ladle the soup into soup bowls and sprinkle over with the shredded leek.
Serve immediately.

Per Serving: 236kcals, 2.9g Fat.

FRENCH
TARRAGON

Herb and Lemon Pork Chops (Serves 4) ***

4 pork chops (trimmed of fat)
2 tbsp lemon juice
1 tsp oregano
1 tsp thyme
Black pepper (to season)
1 tbsp olive oil

1. Place the chops in a glass baking dish and add the lemon juice, oregano, thyme and a sprinkle of black pepper. Make sure that the chops are all covered with the mixture and leave to marinate for 20 minutes.

2. Place the olive oil in a frying pan and heat over a medium heat. Add the chops and cook for approx. 10 minutes, turning once. Cooking times may vary, depending on the thickness of the chops.

Serve with a choice of vegetables.

Per serving: 165kcals, 6.7g Fat.

Lemon Chicken with Parsley (Serves 8) *****

8 chicken breasts (skinless)
Juice of 2 lemons
25g/1/2 cup of fresh parsley (chopped)
Black pepper (to season)

1. Preheat the oven to 230C/450F/Gas mark 8. Spray a baking tray with low-fat cooking spray (you may need two trays) and lay on the chicken breasts.

2. Drizzle the lemon juice over the chicken and sprinkle with the fresh parsley. Season with black pepper, according to taste.

Place in the oven and cook for 20 minutes.

Per Serving: 154kcals, 1.8g Fat.

Spiced Roast Pork with Peppers (Serves 6) ****

650-700g lean pork fillets (trimmed)
1 orange pepper
1 red pepper
1 yellow pepper
9 tbsp dark soy sauce
3 tbsp dry sherry
2 tbsp red wine vinegar
1 1/2 tsp five-spice powder
2 cloves of garlic (crushed)
1-inch piece fresh ginger (root – finely chopped)
5 tbsp caster sugar
2 spring onions, (shredded – lengthways)
Fresh chives (finely chopped)

1. Place the pork in a shallow glass baking dish. Place the garlic, ginger, soy sauce, sherry and five-spice powder in a bowl and mix together well.

2. Spoon over the pork fillets, cover with baking foil and refrigerate for 1 hour.

3. Preheat the oven to 190C/375F/Gas mark 5. Remove the pork from the fridge and drain the sauce, reserving it at one side.

4. Place the pork on a roasting rack over a roasting pan and place in the oven for 55-60 minutes; basting occasionally with the reserved marinade sauce.

5. Whilst the pork is cooking, halve and deseed the peppers. Cut the peppers into approx. 2cm strips and place them on a baking sheet. Place in the oven for the last 30 minutes cooking time, (alongside the pork).

Spiced Roast Pork with Peppers/Cont.

6. Place the red wine vinegar and caster sugar in a saucepan and heat over a medium heat. Heat until the sugar dissolves and then bring to the boil.

7. Reduce the heat and simmer for 3 minutes, until the mixture is of a syrupy texture.

8. Remove the pork from the oven and brush the syrup over it. Leave to stand for 5-8 minutes, then slice the pork into 1/2 inch slices.

9. Arrange the pork on a serving dish, along with the cooked pepper slices.

Garnish with the shredded spring onions, cucumber and fresh chives.

Per Serving: 282kcals, 5g Fat.

Turkey Chilli (Serves 4-6) ****

450g lean turkey mince
3 carrots (chopped)
1 red pepper (chopped)
150g/2 cups of canned kidney beans (drained & rinsed)
400g salsa
375g/1 & 2/3 canned corn (drained)

1. Preheat the oven to 160C/325F/Gas mark 3. Place the peppers and carrots at the bottom of a 5 litre crockpot, (slow-cook). Add the turkey mince, kidney beans, corn and salsa.

2. Cook on low for 6-7 hours.

Per Serving: 402kcals, 5.2g Fat.

Winter Beef & Vegetable Soup (Serves 4) ****

60g/1/2 cup of pearl barley
1200ml/5 & 1/3 cups of fresh beef stock
1 tsp dried mixed herbs
1 carrot (diced)
1 leek (shredded)
225g lean sirloin beef
1 onion (chopped)
2 tbsp fresh parsley (chopped)

1. Place the pearl barley in a large saucepan.
Add in the beef stock and mixed
herbs.

2. Bring to the boil. Reduce the heat,
cover and simmer for 10 minutes,
(skim away any residue that lies on
the top of the soup with a flat ladle).

3. Trim any fat from the sirloin beef and
cut into thin strips. Add the carrot, leek,
onion, celery and beef into the saucepan of
stock.

4. Bring back to the boil. Reduce the heat, cover and
simmer for about 20 minutes, (until the meat and vegetables are
tender).

5. Skim away any further residue on the surface of the soup. Season with salt and
pepper, according to taste and simmer for a further two minutes.

6. Ladle the soup into serving bowls and sprinkle with fresh chopped parsley. Serve
with crusty bread, if desired.

Per Serving: 161kcals, 3.3g Fat.

Lemony Lamb Chops (Serves 6) ***

6 x 100g lamb loin chops (trimmed)
75ml/1/3 cup of fresh lemon juice
1 tsp oregano
1 tsp thyme
1 tsp ground black pepper

1. Place the lemon, herbs and black pepper in a small bowl and mix together. Place the chops in a shallow glass baking dish and add the marinade. Coat all of the chops well and leave to marinate for 20 minutes.

2. Spray a non-stick frying pan with low-fat cooking and place over a medium/high heat. Add the chops and cook for 4-5 minutes each side, (depending on the thickness of the chops).

Serve with new potatoes and a choice of vegetables.

Per Serving: 165kcals, 6.7g Fat

Spicy Turkey Meatballs (Makes 30) ***

400g/3/4lb lean minced turkey
1 medium onion (finely chopped)
1 jalapeno pepper (finely chopped)
2 egg whites
2/3 cup of dry breadcrumbs
75ml/1/3 cup of skimmed milk
2 tsp ground cumin
2 tsp chili powder
110g/1/2 cup of coriander (finely chopped)

1. Preheat the oven the 200C/400F/Gas mark 6. Spray a baking tray with low-fat cooking spray.

2. Place all the ingredients in a large bowl and mix together well with a fork. Once mixed, make approximately 11/2 inch meatballs and place them on the baking tray.

3. Bake for 20 minutes, turning them over once half-way through cooking.

4. Remove from the oven and transfer to a frying pan, with approximately 4-5 cups of a low-fat marinara sauce.

Serve with whole wheat pasta and a side salad.

Per Serving (with sauce): 232kcals, 7.5g Fat.

Pork Medallions with Cider-Apples (Serves 4) ****

1 green apple (cored & cut into wedges)
1 red apple (cored & cut into wedges)
8 lean pork medallions (trimmed)
150ml/2/3 cup of chicken stock
150ml/2/3 cup of dry cider
2 tsp vegetable oil
1 onion (finely sliced)
1 tsp caster sugar
1 tsp dried sage
1 tbsp lemon juice

1. Tie clean string around each of the pork medallions and set to one side.

2. Place the lemon juice and apple wedges in a bowl and mix together, (this will stop the wedges going brown).

3. Place the oil in a frying pan and heat; add the onion and cook for 4-5 minutes. Add in the sugar and cook for a further 4 minutes, until golden brown.

4. Add the pork and cook on each side for 2-3 minutes. Add the chicken stock, cider and dried sage. Bring to the boil, reduce the heat and leave to simmer for 20 minutes.

5. Add the apple wedges to the pork and mix carefully. Season with salt and pepper, according to taste and cook for a further 4-5 minutes.

6. Remove the string from the pork and serve with a selection of fresh vegetables or salad.

Per Serving: 192kcals, 5.7g Fat.

Beef & Vegetable Gratin (Serves 4) **

350g lean minced beef
4 courgettes (thinly sliced)
1 onion (finely chopped)
2 large tomatoes (thinly sliced)
1 tsp mixed herbs
1 tbsp plain flour
1 tbsp tomato puree
2 tbsp cornflour
150ml/2/3 cup of low-fat fromage frais
300ml/1 & 1/3 cups of skimmed milk
300ml/1 & 1/3 cups of beef stock
1 egg yolk
3 tbsp Parmesan cheese
Salt and pepper (to season)

1. Preheat the oven to 190C/375F/Gas mark 5. Heat up a non-stick frying pan and fry the minced beef and onion for 4 minutes, until slightly brown.

2. Add the flour, stock, herbs, tomato puree and seasoning – stir in well. Bring to the boil. Reduce the heat and simmer for 25-30 minutes.

3. Spoon out the mixture into a ovenproof gratin dish and cover with a layer of tomatoes, followed by a layer of courgettes.

4. Place cornflour and a little of the milk in a small bowl and blend together. Pour the rest of the milk into a saucepan and bring to the boil. Stir in the cornflour/milk mixture and heat through for 1-2 minutes, until thickened.

5. Remove the saucepan from the heat and beat in the egg yolk and low-fat fromage frais. Season as desired.

6. Spoon the mixture evenly over the top layer of courgettes in the gratin dish and sprinkle with Parmesan cheese. Place on a baking tray and place in the oven for 25-30 minutes. Serve with a choice of vegetables.

Per Serving: 319kcals, 10.3g Fat.

Creamy Sweetcorn & Ham Soup (Serves 4) *****

450g/2 cups of canned sweetcorn
4 tbsp low-fat fromage frais
100g lean ham (diced)
2 tbsp fresh chives (finely chopped)
1 tbsp cornflour
3 tbsp cold water
1 onion (chopped)
1 potato (peeled & diced)
900ml/4 cups of skimmed milk
1 bay leaf
1/2 tsp ground nutmeg
Salt and pepper (to season)

1. Place the potato and onion in a large saucepan and add in the skimmed milk. Add the nutmeg, bay leaf and half of the sweetcorn.

2. Place over a medium/high heat and bring to simmering point. Reduce the heat, cover and gently simmer for 15 minutes; stirring occasionally. Be careful not to burn the milk.

3. Remove from the heat and discard the bay leaf. Leave to cool for 10-15 minutes.

4. Transfer the liquid to a blender and process for about 6-8 seconds.

5. Pour the liquid back into the large saucepan and place back over a medium heat.

Creamy Sweetcorn & Ham Soup/Cont.

6. Place the cold water and cornflour in a bowl and combine to make a paste. Stir this into the soup mixture.

7. Bring the soup back to simmering point, stirring until it thickens. Add the remaining sweetcorn, season with salt and pepper; and continue to cook for 2-3 minutes.

8. Stir in the fromage frais and cook for 1 minute. Ladle the soup into serving bowls and sprinkle with diced ham and chives. Serve immediately.

Per Serving: 346kcals, 2.4g Fat.

Lean-Beef Shepherd's Pie (Serves 6) ***

450g lean minced beef
225ml/1 cup of beef broth (fat-free)
2 carrots (chopped)
1 onion (chopped)
1 tbsp vegetable oil
150g/1 cup of frozen peas
2 tbsp tomato puree
2 tbsp Worcestershire sauce
2 tsp mixed herbs
5 large white potatoes
1 tbsp low-fat butter
110ml/1/2 cup of skimmed milk

1. Preheat the oven to 200C/400F/Gas mark 6. Heat the vegetable oil in a large saucepan and add the chopped onions and carrots. Sauté gently until softened.

2. Add the minced beef and cook on a higher heat, until slightly browned. Stir in the tomato puree, broth, herbs and Worcestershire sauce.

3. Reduce the heat and simmer for 12-15 minutes. Stir in the frozen peas and simmer for a further 5 minutes.

4. Whilst the sauce is cooking, bring a large saucepan of water to the boil and add the potatoes. Reduce the heat and simmer for 15-20 minutes, (depending on the size of the potatoes).

5. Drain the potatoes and add the butter and milk. Mash well until smooth and creamy. Pour the beef mixture into a baking dish and leave for 6-8 minutes.

6. Spread the mashed potato evenly over the top. Season with black pepper, if desired.

7. Place in the oven for 20-25 minutes. Serve with choice of vegetables.

Per Serving: 322kcals, 7.6g Fat.

Minty Lamb Burgers (Serves 8) ***

Burgers & Buns:

700g lean lamb mince

2 small onions (finely chopped)

Salt & pepper (to season)

8 tbsp dry wholemeal breadcrumbs

4 tbsp mint jelly

4 tomatoes (sliced)

8 large lettuce leaves

8 wholemeal baps (sliced open)

Mint Relish:

8 tbsp low-fat fromage frais

2 tbsp mint jelly

4 inch piece cucumber
(finely chopped)

1 1/2 tbsp fresh mint
(finely chopped)

Burgers:

1. Place the lamb mince in a large mixing bowl and add the breadcrumbs, mint jelly and onion. Mix in well with a fork and season, to taste.

2. Once mixed well, mould the mixture with your hands and divide into 8 equal sized 'patties'. Place on a plate and refrigerate for 25-30 minutes.

3. Preheat the grill to a medium heat and line the grill tray with parchment paper; making sure to tuck the ends in under the grill rack.

4. Whilst the burgers are cooking, place the fromage frais, chopped cucumber, mint jelly and chopped mint in a bowl and mix together well. Cover and leave in the refrigerator until required.

5. Once the burgers are cooked, place them with absorbent kitchen towel and turn them, in order to soak up any excess fat.

6. Serve the burgers inside the wholemeal baps, with the cucumber slices, tomato, lettuce and top with the mint relish. Serve immediately.

Per Serving: 237kcals, 7.8g Fat.

Turkey & Fruit Curry (Serves 4) ***

450g turkey breast (skinless & diced)
300ml/1 & 1/3 cups of fresh chicken stock
1 onion (chopped)
3 tbsp mild curry paste
1 tbsp vegetable oil
55g/1/4 cup of sultanas
375g/1 & 2/3 cups of canned apricot halves
(drained, but reserve a little juice)
1 green chilli (deseeded & sliced)
125g/3/4 cup of frozen peas
335g/1 1/2 cups of basmati rice
4 tbsp fresh coriander (chopped)
1 fresh apricot for garnish (optional)

1. Cook the basmati rice, as per the packet instructions. Heat the oil in a large non-stick saucepan and add the onion and turkey.

2. Gently fry for 5-6 minutes, until the turkey is golden brown. Add the curry paste, coating the turkey well. Pour in the chicken stock and bring to the boil, stirring continuously. Reduce the heat and simmer for 15 minutes.

Turkey & Fruit Curry/Cont.

3. Add the frozen peas and return to the boil. Reduce the heat, cover the pan and simmer for a further 5 minutes.

4. Cut the apricots into thick slices and add to the saucepan. Stir in the raisins.

5. Add some of the reserved apricot juice if the contents are becoming dry. Cook for 2-3 minutes.

6. Mix the cooked rice with the fresh coriander and sliced chilli. Serve onto plates and top with the curry. Add slices of fresh apricot to garnish.

Serve immediately.

Per Serving: 418kcals, 7.9g Fat.

Turkey Meatloaf (Serves 4 – 8 Slices) ****

400g/14 oz lean turkey mince
40g/3/4 cup of plain breadcrumbs
55ml/1/4 cup of skimmed milk
1/4 cup of egg substitute
1/2 onion (chopped)
1 small carrot (chopped)
40g/1/2 cup of sliced mushrooms (finely chopped)
1 clove of garlic
1/2 tbsp Worcestershire sauce
2 tbsp of tomato ketchup

1. Preheat the oven to 200C/400F/Gas mark 6. Line a large rimmed baking tray with baking paper or baking foil.

2. Place the milk and breadcrumbs in a bowl and leave to soak for 2-3 minutes.

3. Place the garlic, onions and carrots in food processor and process with the grater attachment. Transfer the grated ingredients to a large bowl and add the finely chopped mushrooms

4. Gradually mix in the turkey mince with the vegetables and mix well. Add in the breadcrumb mixture and mix together well with a fork.

Turkey Meatloaf/Cont.

5. Add the Worcestershire sauce, ketchup and egg substitute and mix together carefully with fingers. Form a loaf shape on the baking tray, approx. 7.5 x 4 inches.

6. Place in the oven and bake for 55-60 minutes. Remove from the oven when cooked and leave for 8-10 minutes before slicing.

Per Slice: 108kcals, 3.7g Fat.

Low Fat 'Stars' Key for recipes

0 – 2.9g Fat	=	*****
3g – 5.9g Fat	=	****
6g – 8.9g Fat	=	***
9.0g – 12.9g Fat	=	**
13g+ Fat	=	*

Baked Haddock and Tomato (Serves 4) ****

4 x 100g haddock fillets
1 tsp dried onion
450g/2 cups of canned chopped tomatoes
110ml/1/2 cup of fresh lime juice
1 tsp dried parsley

1. Preheat the oven to 200C/400F/Gas mark 6. Place the tomatoes, parsley, lime juice and onion in a jug and mix well.

2. Place the fish fillets in a shallow glass dish. Pour the liquid mixture over the fish.

3. Place in the oven (uncovered) and bake for 20 minutes. Remove from the oven and serve.

Per Serving: 149kcals, 3g Fat.

Roasted Spiced Salmon (Serves 8) ***

8 x 100g salmon fillets
1 1/2 tbsp chili powder
1 1/2 tsp paprika
Juice of 1 lemon
1 1/2 tbsp cumin
Ground black pepper

1. Preheat the oven to 220C/425F/Gas mark 7. Line 2 baking trays with baking paper and spray with low-fat cooking spray.

2. Place the spices in a small bowl and mix together well. Place 4 each of the salmon fillets, (skin side down), on each of the baking trays. Sprinkle over the spices and then rub them gently.

3. Squeeze the lemon juice equally over each of the fillets and sprinkle lightly with the ground black pepper.

4. Place in the oven for 10-12 minutes, (per inch of fillet thickness). Remove from the oven when the fish flakes easily with a fork.

Per Serving: 179kcals, 7.4g Fat.

*Shrimp in Coconut (Serves 8) ****

550g shrimp (peeled, deveined – with tail)
335ml/1 1/2 cups of coconut milk (light option)
4 cups of brown rice
4 tsp fish sauce
4 tbsp reduced-fat smooth peanut butter (softened)
4 tsp brown sugar
1 tbsp freshly grated ginger
200g/2 cups of baby spinach (chopped)
25g/1/2 cup of coriander (chopped)

1. Cook the rice as per the packet instructions, (time this in with the end of cooking the shrimp).

2. Place the peanut butter, coconut milk, brown sugar, ginger and fish sauce in a bowl and whisk together.

3. Spray a non-stick frying pan and heat over a medium heat. Add the shrimp and cook for 2-3 minutes, until they turn pink.

4. Pour the coconut milk mixture over the shrimps and sprinkle over the chopped spinach and coriander.

5. Cook for 2-3 minutes until the mixture thickens. Serve immediately with the brown rice.

Per Serving: 286kcals, 7.9g Fat.

Shrimp-ed Spaghetti (Serves 8) ****

900g shrimp (deveined)
450g whole wheat spaghetti
450g/2 cups of canned chopped tomatoes (in puree)
2 cloves of garlic (crushed)
225g/1 cup of onion (finely chopped)
225g tomato puree
2 tbsp fresh basil (chopped)
2 tsp olive oil
1 tsp oregano

1. Cook the spaghetti as per the packet instructions, (time in with the end of cooking the shrimp).

2. Whilst the spaghetti is cooking, place the olive oil in a large non-stick frying pan and place over a medium heat.

3. Add in the onion and garlic and fry for 3-4 minutes, until softened.

4. Add in the tomato puree and chopped tomatoes and sprinkle in some oregano. Simmer gently for 10-15 minutes, until the sauce begins to reduce and thicken. Stir in the shrimp and heat well for 5-6 minutes.

5. Drain the pasta and add the sauce and shrimps, toss well. Serve and sprinkle with the chopped basil.

Per Serving: 377kcals, 3.2g Fat.

Grilled Cajun Red Snapper (Serves 4) ****

550g red snapper fillets (divided into 4)
2 tsp olive oil
2 tbsp Cajun seasoning
Juice of 1 lime
Juice of 1 lemon

1. Place the lemon juice, lime juice, olive oil and Cajun seasoning in a bowl, (large enough to take the fillets) and mix together well.

2. Place the red snapper fillets in the bowl and cover well with the dressing. Cover and place in the refrigerator to marinate for 30 minutes.

3. Heat the grill to a medium setting and spray the grill pan with low-fat cooking spray.

4. Lay the fillets on the grill pan and place under the grill for 6-8 minutes, (depending on the thickness of the fillets.)

Season with pepper and herbs if desired.

Per Serving: 168kcals, 4.2g Fat.

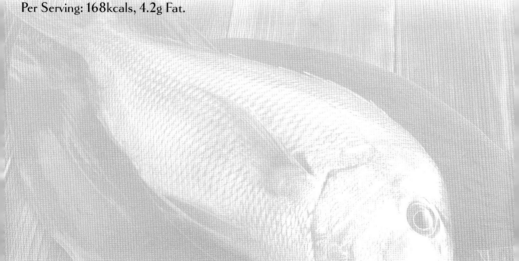

Cod Fillets: Mediterranean Cod (Serves 4) *****

450g cod fillets (cut into 4 portions)
75ml/1/3 cup of dry white wine
1 onion (finely chopped)
1 courgette (thinly sliced)
110g/1/2 cup of baby spinach
110g/1/2 cup of Portabello mushrooms (sliced)
450g/2 cups of canned crushed tomatoes
2 tbsp fresh lemon juice
1 tsp oregano

1. Preheat the oven to 220C/425F/Gas mark 7. Place the spinach and onions at the bottom of a baking dish and lay the cod fillets over the top.

2. Place the mushrooms and courgettes over the top of the fish and add the tomatoes, white wine, lemon juice and oregano.

3. Cover the dish and place in the oven for 20 minutes, until the fish flakes easily with a fork.

Per Serving: 175kcals, 1.3g Fat.

Cod-Fish Pie (Serves 6) *****

450g/1 lb cod fillet (cut into 4 pieces)
110g/1/2 cup of onion (finely chopped)
225ml/1 cup of skimmed milk
225g/1 cup of frozen peas
110g/1/2 cup of sweet corn
1 tbsp cornstarch (dissolved in 1/4 cup of water)
1/4 cup of fresh parsley (finely chopped)
Black pepper (to season)
900g/4 cups of white potatoes (peeled & cut into 1 1/2 inch pieces)
1 tbsp low-fat butter
110ml/1/2 cup of skimmed milk

1. Preheat the oven to 200C/400F/Gas mark 6. Boil the potato pieces for about 15-20 minutes. Whilst the potatoes are boiling, place the skimmed milk in a frying pan and simmer.

2. Add in the chopped onion and season with the pepper, according to taste. Place the cod fillets into the frying pan, (being careful not to splash). Cook on a low/medium heat for about 10 minutes, until the fish begins to flake easily with a fork.

3. Remove the fish from the frying pan and place in a 8 x 8 baking dish. Cut the fish into small chunks and sprinkle with the peas, sweet corn and parsley.

4. Add the dissolved cornstarch to the frying pan and stir in well. Cook on a low heat until the mixture has thickened and then pour over the fish/vegetable mix.

5. Drain the potatoes of water, add some more skimmed milk and the low-fat butter and mash until smooth and creamy. Spread the mash over the top of the fish/vegetables and fluff with a fork.

6. Place in the oven and bake for 20 minutes, until the top is golden brown.

Per Serving: 240kcals, 2g Fat.

Grilled Tuna & Rice Stuffed Peppers (Serves 8) ***

620g/2 3/4 cups of canned sweetcorn
225g/1 cup of low-fat grated cheddar cheese
115g/1 cup of wild rice
115g/1 cup of brown rice
450g/2 cups of canned tuna chunks (drained & flaked)
8 red bell peppers
1 bunch fresh basil (shredded)
2 tbsp grated Parmesan cheese
4 tbsp white breadcrumbs
Salt and pepper (to season)

1. Cook both of the different rice, in different pans, according to the packet instructions. Drain and rinse well.

2. Whilst the rice is cooking, halve and deseed the peppers. Arrange on a clean grill with the cut-side facing down.

3. Place under a medium grill and cook for 4-5 minutes. Remove from the grill and turn over; return to the grill and cook for a further 4-5 minutes.

4. Transfer both lots of cooked and drained rice to a bowl. Add in the tuna flakes and sweetcorn; mix together well. Add in the grated cheese, basil leaves and season, according to taste. Mix well.

5. Divide the mixture evenly into each pepper half. Place the Parmesan and breadcrumbs in a bowl and mix. Sprinkle over each of the peppers.

6. Place the peppers back under the grill for 4-5 minutes and cook until golden brown. Serve immediately with a green salad.

(To lower the fat content, leave out the Parmesan cheese and breadcrumb mix.)

Per Serving: 383kcals, 6.8g Fat.

Cod Fillets and Lentils (Serves 4) ****

550g cod fillet (cut into 4 pieces)
225g/1 cup of lentils (picked through & rinsed)
1 clove of garlic (crushed)
225g/1 cup of onion (chopped)
375g/1 & 2/3 cup of canned chopped tomatoes
225ml/1 cup of vegetable broth
2 tsp olive oil
10g/1/3 cup of fresh parsley (chopped)

1. Place the olive oil in a non-stick frying pan and heat over a medium heat. Add the onions and sauté for 3-4 minutes.

2. Add the lentils, tomatoes and vegetable broth. Bring to the boil, reduce the heat and simmer for 25 minutes.

3. Add the fish pieces and cover the pan. Cook for a further 8-10 minutes, until the fish flakes easily with a fork. Serve immediately.

Per Serving: 358kcals, 4g Fat.

Mediterranean Fish Soup (Serves 4) ****

450g cod fillets (cut into 1 inch cubes)
450g fresh mussels (washed/prepared)
225g fresh peeled shrimp prawns
450g/2 cups of canned chopped tomatoes
1 tbsp olive oil
1 onion (chopped)
2 cloves of garlic (crushed)
450ml/2 cups of fresh fish stock
110ml/1/2 cup of dry white wine
1 bay leaf
1/2 tsp thyme
1/2 tsp rosemary
1/2 tsp oregano
Salt & pepper to season

1. Heat the olive oil in a large saucepan and add the onion and garlic. Sauté for 2-3 minutes.

2. Add in the wine and fish stock and bring to the boil. Add the cod and mussels, along with the herbs and bay leaf. Reduce the heat, cover and simmer for 5 minutes.

3. Add in the prawns and tomatoes, stirring them in well. Season with salt and pepper, according to taste; cover and continue to cook for a further 4-5 minutes.

4. Remove the bay leaf from the soup, as well as any mussels that haven't opened up, (do not attempt to open them).

5. Ladle the soup into serving bowls and serve with lemon wedges; and crusty bread, if desired.

Per Serving: 271kcals, 5.3g Fat.

Latin-Spice Sole (Serves 4) *****

1 cup of canned black beans (washed & drained)
1 red pepper (chopped)
1 Jalapeno pepper (chopped)
1 tbsp flat parsley
4 sole fillets
2 tbsp tomato puree
1 1/2 tsp oregano

1. Preheat the oven to 200C/400F/Gas mark 6. Spoon the can of black beans into the bottom of a glass baking dish and stir in the chopped jalapeno pepper and red pepper. Mix well, so that the ingredients are evenly distributed.

2. Rub the parsley over the sole fillets and place over the top of the bean mix. Spread a layer of tomato puree over the fish and sprinkle lightly with the oregano.

3. Place in the oven and bake for 15-20 minutes.

Per serving: 228kcals, 1.8g Fat

Tuna Steak with Lime (Serves 4) ****

4 trimmed tuna steaks (6oz each)
1 tsp cumin
2 tsp olive oil
1 tsp ground coriander
1 clove of garlic (crushed)
1/2 tsp grated lime rind
1 tbsp lime juice
Black pepper (to season)
1 tbsp chopped fresh coriander
4 wedges of lime

1. Place the olive oil, garlic, lime rind, ground coriander, cumin and black pepper in a bowl and mix together. Spread the mixture thinly on both sides of the tuna steaks.

2. Heat a non-stick ridged frying pan on a high heat and add the steaks, pressing them down to seal them. Reduce the heat and cook for 4-5 minutes. Turn the steaks over and cook for the same time again.

3. Transfer to serving plates and sprinkle over with chopped coriander and lime juice. Serve with a green salad.

Per Serving: 200kcals, 3.5g Fat.

Tuna Rice Salad (Serves 6) ****

200g canned tuna chunks
1 cup of canned chickpeas
110g/1/2 cup of cherry tomatoes (halved)
75g/1/3 cup of red onion (chopped)
230g/2 cups of brown rice (cooked)
300g/1 & 1/3 cup of artichoke hearts (drained & chopped)
1 1/2 tbsp fresh parsley (chopped)
Juice of 1 lemon
1 tbsp extra virgin olive oil
1 tbsp water

1. Place the lemon juice, olive oil and water in a bowl and whisk together.

2. Place the artichokes, chickpeas, onion, tuna, tomatoes and rice in a bowl and mix together well.

3. Drizzle the dressing over the salad and sprinkle over with chopped parsley. Place in the refrigerator for 2-3 hours before serving.

Per Serving: 212kcals, 4g Fat.

Low Fat 'Stars' Key for recipes

0 – 2.9g Fat	=	*****
3g – 5.9g Fat	=	****
6g – 8.9g Fat	=	***
9.0g – 12.9g Fat	=	**
13g+ Fat	=	*

Mexican Pinto Beans and Rice (Serves 6) *****

150g/1 cup of onions (chopped)
115g/1 cup of long grain white rice
100g/1 cup of celery (chopped)
1 tsp olive oil
1 clove of garlic (crushed)
8oz tin of pinto beans (drained & washed)
170g/3/4 cup of tomato puree
110ml/1/2 cup of water
1 tsp chilli powder
1/4 tsp hot pepper sauce

1. Cook the rice, as per the packet
instructions. Whilst the rice is cooking, heat
the olive oil in a frying pan and add in the
garlic, onions and celery.

2. Cook for
5-6 minutes,
stirring
frequently.

Mexican Pinto Beans and Rice/Cont.

3. Add in the tomato puree, pinto beans, water, hot pepper sauce and chilli powder.

4. Heat through thoroughly for about 10 minutes, stirring occasionally. Serve over the rice, when ready.

Per Serving: 206kcal, 1g Fat.

Vegetable Lasagne (Serves 8) ****

225g dried lasagne sheets
1 butternut squash (chopped)
1 courgette (chopped)
1 carrot (diced)
140g/2 cups of mushrooms (sliced)
1 celery stalk (chopped)
1 onion (finely chopped)
1 clove of garlic (crushed)
2 tins of chopped tomatoes
2 tbsp tomato puree
1 tsp oregano
1 tsp mixed herbs
2 handfuls of spinach (chopped)
2 tsp olive oil
450g/2 cups of low-fat ricotta cheese (or quark)
75g/3/4 cup of low-fat mozzarella cheese

1. Preheat the oven to 190/375F/Gas mark 5. Spray a 11 x 7 inch baking dish with low-fat cooking spray.

2. Place the olive oil in a large saucepan and place over a medium heat. Add the garlic and onion and sauté for 2-3 minutes.

3. Add the celery, mushrooms, carrots, courgettes and squash and gently sauté for approximately 10 minutes, until the vegetables have softened.

4. Add in the tomato puree, chopped tomatoes, herbs and black pepper.

5. Bring to the boil, reduce the heat and simmer for 10 minutes. Stir in the spinach.

6. Spoon a cup of the sauce on the base of the baking dish. Top with a layer of lasagne sheets, followed by a layer of ricotta cheese, (or quark). Add another layer of sauce, followed by lasagne sheets and ricotta cheese.

7. Continue this process and end with a layer of sauce. Top with the mozzarella cheese. Place in the oven and bake for 30 minutes.

Per Serving: 303kcals, 4.1g Fat.

Marinara Linguine (Serves 6) ***

900g fresh linguine
14 tomatoes (cut into 1-inch chunks)
4 cloves of garlic (crushed)
4 tbsp tomato puree
3 tbsp olive oil
1 tbsp fresh basil
1tbsp oregano (finely chopped)
3/4 tsp salt
11/2 sweet onions (finely chopped)**
Grated mozzarella

** Sweet onions are available in the UK between July and September.

1. Add 1 tbsp olive oil to a pan and heat. Add in the onions and sauté for 3-5 minutes, until tender. Add the crushed garlic and cooking, stirring continuously for 30 seconds.

2. Add in the tomato puree and tomatoes and stir in well. Bring to the boil and simmer for 15 minutes, stirring intermittently.

3. Towards the end of the 15 minutes, cook the linguine as per the packet instructions, (3-4 minutes if fresh). Drain and place on a large serving dish.

4. Remove the tomato sauce from the heat and stir in the fresh basil, oregano and 2 tbsp olive oil. Pour over the linguine and serve.

Sprinkle with mozzarella.

Per serving: 450kcals, 7g fat.

Crunchy-Vegetable Spaghetti (Serves 4) *****

Spaghetti:
300g/1 & 1/3 cups of spaghetti
2 carrots (peeled & sliced julienne)
2 medium leeks (trimmed & finely shredded)
150g/1 cup of celeriac (peeled & sliced julienne)
1 red pepper (deseeded & sliced)
1 yellow pepper (deseeded & sliced)
2 cloves of garlic (crushed)
1 tsp celery seeds
1 tbsp lemon juice

Lemon Dressing:
1 tbsp lemon juice
1 tsp finely grated lemon rind
2 tbsps snipped chives
4 tbsps low-fat fromage frais
Salt & pepper (to season)

1. Place all of the vegetables in a large bowl and add the celery seeds and lemon juice. Toss well, coating all the vegetables well.

Crunchy-Vegetable Spaghetti/Cont.

2. Cook the spaghetti, as per the packet instructions. Drain and mix in a little olive oil, (to stop it sticking together). Keep warm.

3. Whilst the spaghetti is cooking, place the vegetables in a steamer or sieve and place over a pan of boiling water.

4. Cover and steam for 5-7 minutes, or until the vegetables are just tender. Place the lemon dressing ingredients in a bowl and mix together well.

5. Transfer the spaghetti and vegetables into a warmed serving bowl and mix together well with the dressing. Serve immediately.

Per Serving: 330kcals, 2.5g Fat.

Red Pepper Pasta (Serves 4) ****

2 x 12oz jars of roasted red sweet peppers (drained)
225g penne pasta
3 cloves garlic (crushed)
3/4 cup of fresh basil
2 tsp virgin olive oil
225ml/1 cup of water
110g/1/2 cup of tomato puree
2 tbsp red wine vinegar
Fresh grated Parmesan cheese (optional)

1. Heat the olive oil in a frying pan and heat over a medium/high heat and sauté the onions until golden brown.

2. Place half the crushed garlic and half of the red peppers in a food processor and blend until the mixture is almost smooth.

3. Add in half of the basil, tomato puree, water and red wine vinegar and blend until the mixture is almost smooth. Pour the mixture into a saucepan.

4. Add the remaining garlic, basil, peppers, tomato puree, tomato puree, water and red wine vinegar to the blender and process, as before. Pour into the saucepan with the other sauce mixture. Cook over a medium heat for 10 minutes, whilst cooking the pasta in another saucepan, (cook as per packet instructions).

5. Drain the pasta and remove the sauce from the heat. Pour over the pasta and serve. Sprinkle over with fresh Parmesan cheese, if desired.

Per Serving: 303kcals,
3g Fat.

Tuscan Vegetable and Bean Soup (Serves 8) *****

4 courgettes (diced)
750g/3 & 1/3 cups of canned mixed beans/pulses
2 tsp dried oregano
2250ml/10 cups of vegetable stock
1 large onion (chopped)
1 clove of garlic (crushed)
2 carrots (chopped)
2 sticks of celery (sliced)
845g/33/4 cups of canned chopped tomatoes
300ml/1 & 1/3 cup of dry red wine
11/2 tbsp tomato puree
Salt and pepper (to season)
Low-fat grated Parmesan cheese (optional)

1. Place the garlic, carrot, onion and celery in a large saucepan and mix together. Add in the vegetable stock, red wine, tomatoes and oregano. Heat over a medium/high heat and bring to the boil.

2. Reduce the eat, cover and simmer for 15 minutes. Add in the mixed beans/pulses and courgettes, cover and continue to simmer for 5 minutes.

3. Add the tomato puree and season with salt and pepper, according to taste. Cook for a further 3-4 minutes, but do not boil.

4. Ladle the soup into serving bowls and sprinkle with Parmesan cheese, if desired.

Per Serving: 156kcals, 1.5g Fat.

Low Fat 'Stars' Key for recipes

0 – 2.9g Fat	=	*****
3g – 5.9g Fat	=	****
6g – 8.9g Fat	=	***
9.0g – 12.9g Fat	=	**
13g+ Fat	=	*

Summer Fruit Brules (Serves 8) ***

900ml/4 cups of summer fruits (strawberries, redcurrants, raspberries, etc)
300ml/1 & 1/3 cups of low-fat natural yoghurt
300ml/1 & 1/3 cups of soured cream
8 tbsp demerara sugar
2 tsp vanilla extract

1. Equally divide the summer fruits between 8 heatproof ramekin dishes.

2. Place the fromage frais, soured cream and vanilla extract in a bowl and mix together well. Spoon the mixture over the fruit, covering the fruit completely.

3. Top each with a serving of 1 tablespoon of demerara sugar and place under a hot grill for 3-4 minutes, until the sugar begins to caramelise. Remove from the grill and leave to cool for 2 minutes before serving.

Per Serving: 165kcals, 7g Fat.

Fruit Muffins (Makes 20) *****

460g/4 cups of self-raising wholemeal flour
2 eggs (beaten)
620ml/23/4 cups of skimmed milk
3 tsp baking powder
55ml/1/2 cup of light muscovado sugar
150g/2/3 cup of dried apricots (finely chopped)
25g/1/4 cup of raisins
2 bananas (mashed)
2 tbsp orange juice
3 tbsp corn oil
2 tsp orange rind (finely grated)
4 tbsp porridge oats

1. Preheat the oven to 200C/400F/Gas mark 6. Line 2 cupcake baking trays with 20 paper muffin cases.

2. Sift the baking powder and flour into a large bowl and stir in the sugar, raisins and chopped apricots.

3. Make a well in the centre of the ingredients and add the milk, eggs, banana, oil and orange rind. Mix together well.

4. Spoon the mixture into the muffin liners, up to about 3/4 full. Sprinkle over the top with the porridge oats.

5. Place in the centre of oven for 30 minutes, until risen and firm to touch.

6. Remove from the oven and leave to cool for 5 minutes. Remove the cupcakes from the baking tray and place on a wire rack to cool.

Per Serving: 180kcals, 1.5g Fat.

Almost-Innocent Brownies (Makes 32) *****

115g/1 cup of flour
100g/1 cup of unsweetened cocoa powder
1 tsp baking powder
225g/1 cup of sugar
2 eggs (lightly beaten)
4 egg whites
225ml/1 cup of unsweetened applesauce
1/4 tsp salt
3 tbsp vegetable oil
4 tsp vanilla extract

1. Preheat the oven to 180C/350F/Gas mark 4. Spray two 8 x 8 inch baking trays with low-fat cooking spray.

2. Place the sugar, flour, cocoa powder, salt and baking powder in a bowl and mix together.

3. In a separate bowl, place the applesauce, oil, egg, egg whites and vanilla extract and mix together. Gradually add in the flour mix, stirring in a little at a time until well combined.

4. Pour into the baking trays and place in the oven for 20 minutes. Remove from the oven and leave to cool for 5-10 minutes. Cut each into 16 equal squares.

Per Serving (per brownie): 74kcals, 2.4g Fat.

Cherry-Chocolate Smoothie (Makes 8 glasses) *****

2 ripe, frozen bananas (sliced)
900ml/4 cups of cherries (pitted)
11/2 tsp vanilla
785ml/31/2 cups of low-fat chocolate milk

1. Place all of the ingredients into a blender and blend on high until smooth. Pour into 8 glasses and serve immediately, with ice.

Per Serving: 218kcals, 2.5g Fat.

Coffee and Chocolate Mousse (Serves 8) ***

300ml/1 & 1/3 cups of half-fat crème fraiche
8 tsp half-fat crème fraiche (to serve)
4 egg whites
2 tbsp coffee essence
4 tsp cocoa powder
2 tsp low-fat drinking chocolate
4 tsp powdered gelatine
4 tbsp boiling water
4 tbsp caster sugar

1. Place the coffee essence in a bowl. In another bowl, mix together the cocoa powder and drinking chocolate.

2. Divide the crème fraiche equally between both bowls and mix well.

3. Place the gelatine in a bowl with the boiling water to dissolve. Place the bowl to one side.

4. Place the sugar and egg whites in a bowl and whisk until stiff. Divide this mixture between the coffee and chocolate bowls and mix in well.

5. Divide the gelatine between the two bowls and fold in carefully using a metal spoon.

6. Alternate a spoonful of each of the mixtures into dessert glasses, until about 3/4 full and swirl together gently. Place in the refrigerator for 1 hour.

7. When ready to serve, top each with a teaspoon of crème fraiche and dust over lightly with cocoa powder.

Per Serving: 130kcals, 6.5g Fat.

Baked Pears with Cranberries (Serves 4-5) ****

3 ripe pears (peeled & quartered)
75g/1/2 cup of dried cranberries
75ml/1/3 cup of pomegranate juice
30g/1/4 cup of walnuts (chopped)

1. Preheat the oven to 180C/350F/Gas mark 4. Place the pear quarters into a baking dish and pour the pomegranate juice over the top. Sprinkle over the cranberries.

2. Place in the oven for 15-20 minutes, until the pears are tender. Serve with low-fat, or fat-free, vanilla yoghurt, if desired.

Per Serving (without yoghurt): 197kcals, 5g Fat.

Tangy Fruit Fool (Serves 8) *****

845ml/3 3/4 cups of low-fat custard
4 egg whites
2 ripe mangoes (peeled & chopped)
3 passion fruit
4 kiwi fruit (peeled & chopped)
2 bananas (chopped)
4 tbsp lime juice
1 tsp lime rind (finely grated)
1 tsp vanilla extract

1. Place the chopped mango in a food processor and blend until smooth.

2. Place the chopped kiwi and banana into a bowl and add in the lime juice and grated rind. Mix together well.

3. Place the egg whites in a bowl and whisk until stiff. Gently fold in the custard and vanilla extract.

4. In 8 tall dessert glasses, place a layer of chopped fruit, then the mango puree, followed by the custard mixture.

5. Repeat this layering, finishing at the top with the custard mixture.

Tangy Fruit Fool/Cont.

6. Place in the refrigerator for 30 minutes. Halve the passion fruits and scoop out the seeds. Spoon the fruit over the chilled 'fools' and serve.

Per Serving: 170kcals, 0.6g Fat.

Zabaglione (Serves 8) *****

400g/13/4 cups of caster sugar
300ml/1 & 1/3 cups of sweet sherry
10 egg yolks

1. Place the egg yolks in a bowl and add the sugar. Whisk together until the mixture is pale and thick.

2. Place the bowl over a saucepan of boiling water and add the sweet sherry, continuously whisking until the mixture becomes light, frothy and warm.

3. Pour the mixture into 8 dessert glasses. Serve with amaretti biscuits or fresh fruit, if desired.

Per Serving: 158kcals, 1g Fat.

Very-Berry Sorbet (Serves 8) ****

400g/2 cups of strawberries
125g/1 cup of raspberries
100g/1 cup of blueberries
110g/1/2 cup of sugar
110ml/1/2 cup of water

1. Place all the ingredients in a blender and blend on high until smooth. Pour the mixture through a sieve into a freezer-safe container.

2. Place in the refrigerator to freeze for about 2-3 hours. Remove from the freezer about 10 minutes before serving to soften a little.

Per Serving: 83kcals, 3g Fat.

Red Berry Salad with Frothy Sauce (Serves 4) *****

Berry Salad:

200g/1 cup of strawberries (halved)
100g/1 cup of redcurrants (trimmed)
100g/1 cup of cranberries
225ml/1 cup of unsweetened apple juice
150g/2/3 cup of light muscovado sugar
1 cinnamon stick (broken)

Sauce:

1/2 cup of marshmallows
125g/1 cup of raspberries
2 tbsp blackcurrant cordial

Berry Salad:

1. Place the sugar, cranberries, redcurrants, apple juice and cinnamon stick in a saucepan and place over a medium/high heat. Bring to the boil, then reduce the heat and simmer for 8-10 minutes.

2. Add in the strawberries and stir well. Once mixed, remove from the heat and transfer the mixture to a large bowl. Cover and leave to cool for 10 minutes, before transferring the bowl into the refrigerator for 1 hour. On removing the bowl from the refrigerator, discard the cinnamon stick.

Sauce:

3. Place the blackcurrant cordial and raspberries in a saucepan and place over a medium/high heat. Bring to the boil, then reduce the heat and simmer for 3 minutes, until the fruit begins to soften.

4. Add in the marshmallows and heat through, stirring continuously, until the marshmallows melt.

5. Transfer the berry salad into serving bowls and spoon over the warm sauce. Serve immediately.

Per Serving: 220kcals, 0.3g Fat.

Summer Fruit Salad (Serves 6) *****

100g/1/2 cup of strawberries (halved)
50g/1/2 cup of blueberries
60g/1/2 cup of raspberries
50g/1/2 cup of blackberries
100g/1 cup of redcurrants
150g/3/4 cup of caster sugar
6 tbsp low-fat fromage frais
5 tbsp water
Grated rind of 1 orange
Juice of 1 orange
2 tsp arrowroot
2 tbsp port

1. Place the water, grated orange rind and sugar in a saucepan and heat over a medium heat, stirring continuously until the sugar has dissolved.

2. Add the orange juice and redcurrants and bring to the boil. Reduce the heat and simmer for 2-3 minutes.

3. Remove from the heat and drain, reserve the syrup and place the redcurrants in a bowl. Place the arrowroot in a bowl and mix with a little water.

4. Return the reserved syrup to the saucepan and add in the arrowroot. Bring to the boil, stirring continuously until the mixture thickens. Stir in the port, mixing it in well.

5. Pour the syrup over the redcurrants in the bowl and add in the rest of the summer fruits. Mix the fruits together well and leave to cool.

6. Once cooled, serve in dessert dishes with a tablespoon of the low-fat fromage frais.

Per Serving: 110kcals, 0.1g Fat.

Chocolate Cupcakes (Makes 24) *****

170g/1 1/2 cups of flour
60g/1/4 cup of light brown sugar
60g/1/4 cup of sugar
50g/1/2 cup of unsweetened cocoa powder
1 tsp bicarbonate of soda
1/2 tsp baking powder
1 large egg
2 tsp vanilla extract
225ml/1 cup of low-fat buttermilk
1/4 tsp salt
55ml/1/4 cup of unsweetened applesauce (strained)

1. Preheat the oven to 180C/350F/Gas mark 4. Lightly spray 2 x 12-cupcake baking tray with low-fat cooking spray.

2. Place the flour, bicarbonate of soda, baking powder, salt and cocoa powder in a bowl and mix together.

3. In a large separate bowl, place the sugar and egg and beat together well. Add in the applesauce and vanilla extract and stir in.

4. Gradually add the flour mixture and buttermilk, by alternating a little of each and stirring in, (starting and ending with the flour mixture).

5. Spoon the mixture into the cupcake baking tray, to about 3/4 full. Place in the oven and bake for 10-12 minutes.

6. Remove from the oven and leave to cool for 5 minutes, before transferring to a wire cooling rack.

Per Serving (per cake): 74kcals, 0.6g Fat.

Lemon Cake Bars (Makes 32 squares) *****

Topping:

6 tbsp flour
2 eggs
2 egg whites
450g/2 cups of sugar
1/2 tsp baking powder
1/4 tsp salt
Zest & juice of 1 lemon
Sifted icing sugar (to decorate)

Cake base:

230g/2 cups of flour
110g/1/2 cup of sugar
80g/1 cup of quick-cook oats
5 tbsp low-fat butter

1. Preheat the oven 180C/350F/Gas mark 4. Lightly spray two 8 inch square baking pans with low-fat cooking spray.

2. Place the oats, sugar and flour in a bowl and mix together. Using a pastry blender, add in the butter and blend together until the mixture reaches a crumble texture.

3. Divide the mixture between the two baking pans and press to the bases of each. Place in the oven for 10 minutes, until the edges turn golden brown.

4. Whilst the bases are baking, place the eggs and egg whites in a bowl and whisk. Add the sugar and beat together until creamy. Add in thebaking powder, flour, lemon and salt and whisk until smooth.

5. Remove the cooked bases from the oven and pour the lemon mixture equally over them. Return to the oven and bake for 20-25 minutes.

6. Remove from the oven and leave to cool for 10-15 minutes. Transfer to a wire rack to cool completely.

Cut each cake into 16 even squares.

Per Serving (per square): 133kcals, 2.8g Fat.

Gingerbread Cake (Makes 16 squares) ****

1 tsp ground ginger
110ml/1/2 cup of low-fat buttermilk
140g/1 1/4 cups of flour
110g/1/2 cup of sugar
1/2 tsp bicarbonate of soda
110ml/1/2 cup of molasses
55ml/1/4 cup of vegetable oil
1 egg (lightly beaten)

1. Preheat the oven to 180C/350F/Gas mark 4. Spray a 8-inch square baking tray with a low-fat cooking spray. Place the ginger, bicarbonate of soda and flour in a bowl and mix together.

2. In a separate bowl, place the egg, molasses, buttermilk and sugar and mix well. Gradually stir in the flour mixture and stir together well. Pour the mixture into the baking pan and place in the oven for 25 minutes. Remove from the oven and leave to cool for 5-10 minutes before turning out onto a wire cooling rack. Cut into 16 even squares to serve.

Per Serving (per square): 128kcals, 3.9g Fat.

Carrot Cake (Makes 16 Slices) ****

Cake:

115g/1 cup of whole wheat flour
115g/1 cup of flour
4 egg whites
280g/1 1/4 cups of brown sugar
200g/2 cups of shredded carrot
225ml/1 cup of unsweetened applesauce
110ml/1/2 cup of low fat buttermilk
225g/1 cup of canned crushed pineapple (drained)
75g/1/2 cup of raisins
2 tsp bicarbonate of soda
1/4 tsp nutmeg
1/2 tsp allspice
1 tsp vanilla extract

Icing:

250g/2 cups of icing sugar
1/2 tsp vanilla extract
55g/1/4 cup of low-fat cream cheese
1 tsp lemon juice

Carrot Cake/Cont.

1. Preheat the oven to 180C/350F/Gas mark 4. Spray a 13 x 9 inch baking pan with low-fat cooking spray.

Cake:

2. Place the bicarbonate of soda, flours and spices in a bowl and stir together well.

3. In a separate bowl, beat the egg whites until soft peaks form. Add in the sugar, little by little and beat well. Follow with the applesauce, vanilla and buttermilk.

4. Add the wet ingredients to the flour mixture and stir in until just moist. Stir in carrots, raisins and pineapple. Spoon the mixture into the baking pan and place in the oven for 35-40 minutes.

5. Remove from the oven and leave to cool for 5-10 minutes. Turn out onto a wire cooling rack to cool completely.

Icing:

1. Place the cream cheeses, vanilla and lemon juice in a bowl and beat together. Add the icing sugar, stirring it in little by little until reaching a spreading consistency.

2. Spread over the cooled cake and cut into 16 even squares.

Per Serving: 269kcals, 3.3g Fat.